# Getting Things Done

## Book 2

**Tasks for Connecting the Classroom with the Real World**

Yu Tamura

Paul Wicking

Yuri Yokoyama

Masanori Matsumura

Manami Kobayashi

Yoshitaka Kato

*SANSHUSHA*

# Introduction

　この教科書は、様々な課題に英語で取り組むことを通して、みなさんの英語力を高めていくことを目指しています。この本の目的は、みなさんが英語の資格試験で高いスコアを取れるようにすることではありません。教室以外の場所で英語を使うために必要となる力をみなさんに身に付けてもらうことが目的です。

　教科書を有効に活用するために、いくつかのアドバイスをさせてください。

　まず、間違い・誤りを犯すことを恐れないことです。言語学習において、誤りを犯すことは決して悪いことではありません。言語使用に誤りがあることは「学習の過程」で起こる自然なことであるということを覚えておいてください。2点目も誤りを恐れないことに関連していますが、ことばを使って自分以外の他者に意味を伝えることを重視してください。自分の伝えたいことを伝えるために試行錯誤すること、そして、相手が試行錯誤しているときにはそれを理解しようと努めること、この2つが言語学習においては重要です。このためには、できるだけ日本語を使わずに英語でやりとりを継続することも必要です。これが3点目です。そして、4点目として、自分が理解できないと思ったときにそれを相手に伝えることも大事です。学習者同士でやりとりする場合だけではなく、先生が言ったことが理解できないと思ったときも、そのことを伝えてください。

　コミュニケーションがうまくいかない場合、それは理解する側だけの問題ではありません。話し手と聞き手が協力して解決すべき問題として捉えましょう。この教科書では、英語力を伸ばすためのサポートとして、"Getting better at it" というセクションを各ユニットに設けています。このセクションで、自分が学んだことの記録をつけること、自分にとって必要な語彙や表現、文法事項などをメモすることが、次の学習へとつながっていきます。このセクションを活用して、適宜振り返ることによって、自分が使える「装備」を増やしていきましょう。

　巻末には、各ユニットで使える有用な語彙や表現がまとめてありますので、こちらもうまく活用していきましょう。さらに、各ユニットの自己評価欄が設けてあります。自分の成長を記録して定期的に振り返ることによって、自分の伸びている部分や苦手な部分を意識しながら授業に取り組むことができるでしょう。

　最後に、この教科書を通じて、言語を使って課題を解決することに楽しさを覚え、そして、その過程で自分の英語力が伸びていくことを感じてもらえれば、著者一同にとってこの上ない喜びです。

著者一同

# 本書の構成

## 各ユニットについて（全24ユニット）：

### 1 Getting warmed up

各ユニットの最初にあるこのセクションで、トピックの導入があったり、トピックについて考えたりします。楽しみながら取り組みましょう。

### 2 Getting ready

メインタスクのための準備をします。メインタスクで有用な語彙や表現を学んだり、メインタスクで必要となるスキルの練習をしたりします。

### 3 Getting into it *The main task!*

このセクションがメインタスクであり、ユニットの中心です。本書のすべてのタスクは、意味中心で、現実世界の英語使用に沿った形で設計されています。言語を使うことを目的とするのではなく、成果を得るために言語を使うという意識で取り組みましょう。

### 4 Getting better at it *Language focus*

振り返りは学習を進めていく上で欠かすことができないものです。このセクションでは、タスク遂行中に気づいた自分の言語能力の足りない部分であったり、次にタスクに取り組む際に役に立つ単語や表現をメモします。空欄があるので、授業で指導された注意事項や文法、言語表現についてそのスペースにメモすることができます。

### 5 Getting further *Extension*

このポストタスクでは、メインタスクと同じようなタスクに再度挑戦することで、メインタスクで学んだスキルや言語を活用します。または、タスクのメインテーマを発展させるような活動に取り組むユニットもあります。

### 6 Getting it done *Wrap up*

この最後のセクションは、他の学習者との直接的なやりとりを必要としないタスクです。多くの場合、ライティング課題になっています。よって、状況に応じて授業中に行うことも、宿題として取り組むことも可能です。

## 巻末の便利素材：

### • Self-assessment rubrics

自己評価用のルーブリックです。自己評価を通して、自身の学習を振り返り、自分の弱点や学習の進捗状況を把握したりすることができます。

### • Useful words and expressions

それぞれのユニットのメインタスクをこなすのに便利な単語や表現が掲載されています。

## 先生方へ

　この教科書は、タスクベースの言語指導（Task-based Language Teaching）の理念に基づいて編纂された教科書、『Getting Things Done［Book 1］』の続編です。タスク・ベースの言語指導とは、タスク（現実世界において起こる言語使用のプロセスを含む課題）を基盤として言語教育を考えるアプローチであり、応用言語学や第二言語習得研究において近年注目を集めています。従来型の教科書とは異なり、「覚えて、練習して、使う」というようなプロセスを経るのではなく、学習者が持つリソースを活用させながら言語能力を伸ばしていくという発想に基づいています。

　Book 2 は、Book 1 よりも発展的なタスクを中心に構成されています。したがって、Book 1 よりもレベルの高い学習者におすすめです。Book 1 と同じ素材を扱っているユニットもいくつかありますが、多くの場合よりチャレンジングな内容に作り変えられています。Book 1 で英語を学んだ学習者であれば、多くの課題は馴染みがあるものであり、なおかつ手順に慣れているため、より英語を使うことに集中して取り組むことができるでしょう。Book 1 を体験していない学習者にとっても、すべての課題が新鮮で、彼らの学習意欲をかきたてるでしょう。

### タスクの分類について

本教科書に掲載されているのは、主に 5 つのタスクです。

- **情報伝達**（Conveying information: CI）　　Unit 1 ～ 8
- **情報合成**（Synthesizing elements: SE）　　Unit 9 ～ 13
- **ナレーション**（Narrating stories: NS）　　Unit 14, 15
- **問題解決**（Solving problems: SP）　　Unit 16 ～ 19
- **意思決定**（Making decisions: MD）　　Unit 20 ～ 24

　**情報伝達**型のタスクは、自分が知っていることを相手は知らない、逆に相手が知っていることを自分は知らないという状態置かれ、その状況で自分の情報を相手に伝え、相手から自分の知らない情報を引き出すことによって何らかの発見や理解といった目的を達成するタイプのタスクです。**情報合成**型は、俯報の伝達だけではなく、パズルのピースを組み合わせるように部分的な情報を組み合わせて一つの全体像を導き出すような課題です。**ナレーション**型はその名の通り、ストーリー性のある一連の絵や動画を見ながらその内容を知らない人に伝えるものです。**問題解決**型は、なんらかの問題状況が提示され、それらについての解答を他者と協力して導き出すものです。最後の**意思決定**型は与えられた候補の中から選択をしたり、優先順位をつけたりすることが求められます。学習者同士の多様な意見を巣約し、最終的に活動に参加している全員が導き出された結論に合意することが必要です。問題解決型では基本的に答えが決まっているのに対して、意思決定型では何が正しいのかについての決まりはなく、自由な発想が許容されています。

　情報伝達、情報合成、ナレーションという 3 つのタイプは、基本的に伝えるべき情報は何らかの形ですでに学習者に与えられています。よって、学習者はその伝え方を考えることに注力することが予想されます。一方で、問題解決型や意思決定型は学習者が自分の意見やアイデアをまず考え、その上でそれを英語で伝える必要がある分だけ比較的難易度の高い課題だといえます。したがって、初学者であれば前者の 3 タイプによって言語化のプロセスになれさせた上で、徐々に問題解決型や意思決定型のタスクを取り入れるように授業を計画することが推奨されます。

## ユニットの順番が指定されていないことについて

　本書は、Unit 1~24 までの 24 のユニットで構成されており、便宜上ユニットに連番の番号をつけています。しかしながら、必ずしも Unit 1 からはじめて Unit 24 で終わることが意図されているわけではありません。この教科書を採択された先生方に自由にタスクを選んでいただき、対象となる科目や学習者の特性も考慮しながら授業をしていただくことで、本書を最大限に活用できます。もちろん、学習者の意見も取り入れながら、彼ら・彼女らの興味関心にあったユニットを選択していただくことも可能です。

## To the teacher

The content of this book is based on the principles of task-based language teaching (TBLT). Task-based language teaching is an approach to language education that prioritizes tasks, or activities which promote the exchange of information in the target language. Tasks have received a lot of attention in recent years in the fields of applied linguistics and second language acquisition.

Unlike many textbooks up until now which follow the process of "presentation, practice, performance" (PPP), a TBLT approach aims to promote learning achievement by having students activate their own linguistic resources in meaning-focused communication.

### Concerning task types

The tasks in this book are divided into five main types.

- **Conveying information** (CI)　　　Units 1-8
- **Synthesizing elements** (SE)　　　Units 9-13
- **Narrating stories** (NS)　　　Units 14, 15
- **Solving problems** (SP)　　　Units 16-19
- **Making decisions** (MD)　　　Units 20-24

Tasks that are of the **conveying information (CI)** type concern a situation where one learner has a piece of information that the other learner does not have. They then convey their own information, or find out the other person's information, for the purpose of discovery or understanding, in order to complete the goal of the task. The **synthesizing elements (SE)** type of tasks not only involve conveying information, but also require different pieces of information to be combined together like pieces in a puzzle. The **narrating stories (NS)** type tasks, as the name implies, require students to tell a story from a series of pictures or a video. **Solving problems (SP)** tasks, meanwhile, concern a situation where students cooperate together in order to find a solution to some kind of problem. The final task type, **making decisions (MD)**, requires students to make a selection from a set of different options, or rank them in order of priority. To do this, they need to share all their opinions and debate together, eventually agreeing on the best course of action. While SP tasks have a definite answer that is either right or wrong, MD tasks have answers that are free and open and depend upon the particular ideas of each group.

With conveying information (CI), synthesizing elements (SE) and narrating stories (NS) type of tasks, the learners have already been given all the necessary information, in one form or another. Therefore, learners are primarily concentrating on how they will pass on that information. Tasks that involve solving problems (SP) and making decisions (MD) are more cognitively demanding, as learners first need to think of their own opinions and ideas, and then consider how best they can express that in English. Therefore, it is recommended that lower level students first undertake the first three types of tasks, in order to get used to the process of language interaction, before gradually moving on to solving problems and making decisions type tasks.

## Order of units

The units in this book are grouped according to the above task types, numbered from 1 to 24. However, it is not necessary to start at Unit 1 and follow the order until Unit 24. To get the most out of this book, teachers should select the most appropriate units, taking into account the focus of the course and the needs/interests of students.

# Table of Contents

## Unit 1 — Fantastic flags

**Goal** To explain complex designs
説明に基づいて国旗を推測する

### 1 Getting warmed up

**Listen and spot the flag**

1. The teacher is going to describe four of the national flags below. Listen carefully, take notes, and write the letter of the flag that is being described.

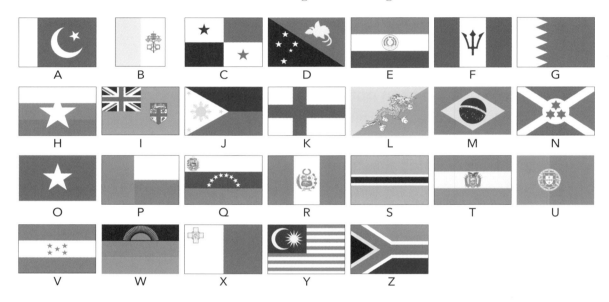

| No. | Notes | Flag letter |
|-----|-------|-------------|
| 1 | | |
| 2 | | |
| 3 | | |
| 4 | | |

2. Compare your answers with a partner.

### 2 Getting ready

**Identify the flag**

Work in a pair. Choose one of the national flags in 1 **Getting warmed up** and describe it to your partner. Your partner will guess and point out the flag. When your partner guesses correctly, swap roles. How many national flags can you identify together?

**Number of correctly identified flags:** _____

## 3 Getting into it

### Describe and draw

Make a group of three. Two students are the 'directors' and the other is the 'drawer'.

**Directors :** Receive a picture of a national flag from the teacher. Do not show it to the drawer! Describe the picture in as much detail as possible, so that the drawer can draw it accurately.

**Drawer :** Do not look at the picture but listen carefully to the description. Draw it in the box below. The picture is a country's national flag.

### Points to note:

1. The directors may look at the drawer's picture. If there are any mistakes or differences, the directors can explain how to fix them.
2. The drawer may not look at the directors' picture. If there is something that you don't understand, you can ask questions to the directors.
3. Both the directors and the drawer may not use gestures. Try and communicate all your questions and ideas in English.

When you have finished, compare the picture you drew with the original picture. Reflect on what was difficult, making some notes in the next section.

**Directors :** Attach your picture here.
**Drawer :** Draw the picture here.

## 4 | Getting better at it Language focus

### Reflection

What are some words or expressions in English that were useful to complete this task?

_____

_____

_____

_____

What are some words or expressions in Japanese that you wanted to use, but couldn't?

_____

_____

_____

_____

Notes

## 5 | Getting further Extension

### Task repetition

1. Now, swap roles and decide the new drawer. You're going to work on the same task you did in 3 **Getting into it** but with a different flag. Before that, discuss how you can improve your performance this time and take notes in the space below.

Notes

2. The new directors will receive a different picture of a national flag and follow the same procedure as 3 **Getting into it**. The new drawer can draw the picture in the box below.

> **_Directors :_** _Attach your picture here._
> **_Drawer :_**   _Draw the picture here._

3. Swap roles again. The new directors will receive a different picture of a national flag and follow the same procedure as **3** **Getting into it**. The new drawer can draw the picture in the box below.

> ***Directors :*** *Attach your picture here.*
> ***Drawer :*** *Draw the picture here.*

## 6 Getting it done  ⟨ Wrap up ⟩

**Write a description**

Look at the national flag of Bhutan and write a description of it, giving as much detail as you can.

# Unit 2 Picture this scene

**Goal** To describe and draw a scene
部屋の中の人物や物を描写したり、聞き取って
その絵を描いたりする

## 1 Getting warmed up

### Identify your classmates

Look around the classroom and write the name of a person who…

…is wearing glasses.

…is standing.

…is writing something in the textbook.

…is looking back.

…looks happy.

…has long hair.

## 2 Getting ready

### Describe and draw a person

PART A

Work in a pair. Each student gets a picture of a person. Do not look at your partner's paper.

***Student A :*** Look at Person A. Describe the person to your partner.

***Student B :*** Listen to your partner's description and draw a picture of that person.

PART B

Now, swap roles.

***Student B :*** Look at Person B. Describe the person to your partner.

***Student A :*** Listen to your partner's description, and draw a picture of the person.

*Draw your picture here:*

## 3  Getting into it

### Describe and draw a scene

PART A

Work in a pair. Each student gets a picture of a scene. *Do not look at your partner's paper.*

***Student A :*** Look at Picture A. Describe the scene to your partner.

Think about:

- objects (shape, size, position, etc.)
- people (appearance, action, clothing, etc.)

***Student B :*** Listen to your partner's description and draw a picture of the scene.

PART B

Now, swap roles.

***Student B :*** Look at Picture B. Describe the scene to your partner.

***Student A :*** Listen to your partner's description and draw a picture of the scene.

*Draw your picture here:*

Attach your picture here.

## Reflection

What are some words or expressions in English that were useful to complete this task?

What are some words or expressions in Japanese that you wanted to use, but couldn't?

_____

_____

_____

_____

_____

_____

_____

_____

Notes

5 **Getting further** ⟨ Extension

## Describe a scene

Imagine that you are watching some people having a meal. It can be a meal in your favourite restaurant, or a meal in your own house. Picture the scene in your mind. What is happening?

1. Write down some keywords to help you describe the scene. Do not write full sentences. Think about:
   - How many people are there?
   - What do they look like?
   - What are they doing?
   - What is on the table?
   - Are there any decorations on the walls? etc.

   Keywords

2. Work in a pair.

**Student A :** Describe the scene in as much detail as possible, so that the drawer can draw it accurately.

**Student B :** Listen carefully to the description. Draw it in the box below.

After Student B finishes drawing the picture, show it to Student A. Student A should give some suggestions to improve the picture. Then, swap roles.

| 6 | **Getting it done** | Wrap up |

### Describe another scene

Think of a scene on your daily commute to school. For example, a scene inside the train you usually ride, or a scene at a pedestrian crossing near school. Describe the scene. Try to include sights, sounds and smells.

## Unit 3 — Putting things in place

**Goal** To put things in their proper places in a picture
絵の中の適切な場所にアイテムを配置する

### 1 | Getting warmed up

**Vocabulary building**

Work in a pair. Look at the picture below and list as many items as you can in the picture. How many items do you know? Are there any items you cannot say in English?

List of items

### 2 | Getting ready

**Listen and draw**

1. Your teacher is going to tell you *three items* to add to the picture above.
   Listen carefully and draw the items in their proper places.
2. Compare your picture with a partner.

The main task!

### 3 | Getting into it

**Describe and draw**

Work in a pair. Student A gets Worksheet A from your teacher. There are *23 more items* in this picture than in the picture printed above.

***Student A :*** Describe as many items as possible.

***Student B :*** Listen carefully and *add all the items* to the picture printed above, drawing them in their proper places.

## 4 Getting better at it Language focus

### Reflection

What are some words or expressions in English that were useful to complete this task?

What are some words or expressions in Japanese that you wanted to use, but couldn't?

Notes

## 5 Getting further Extension

### Task repetition

Now, swap roles. This time:

**Student B :** Close your textbook and get Worksheet B from your teacher. Try and remember all the 23 items you drew in the picture in your textbook. Describe the items and their locations to your partner.

**Student A :** Listen carefully and check the items on Worksheet A that Student B was able to describe.

## 6 Getting it done Wrap up

### Write about locations

Choose five items from the complete picture and write sentences to describe their locations.

1.

2.

3.

4.

5.

Attach your picture here.

# Unit 4 | Spot the difference

**Goal** To identify the differences between two pictures
絵を見せ合うことなく2つの絵の間の相違点をできるだけ多く見つける

## 1 Getting warmed up

**Listen and spot the differences**

Look at the picture below. The teacher will describe a picture that is similar to this one. Listen carefully. How many differences can you find?

## 2 Getting ready

**Vocabulary building**

1.  Get a picture from your teacher. Do not look at other students' pictures. Are there any words and expressions that you need to describe your picture, but you don't know in English? Choose *six words or expressions* and write them down below.

_____     _____

_____     _____

2.  Compare your vocabulary list with a partner who has the same picture. Among the words that your partner wrote, write down *three words* that are the most helpful to describe your picture.

_____     _____

## 3 Getting into it

Work with your partner and *find 10 differences.*

## 4 | Getting better at it — Language focus

### Reflection

What are some words or expressions in English that were useful to complete this task?

_____

_____

_____

_____

What are some words or expressions in Japanese that you wanted to use, but couldn't?

_____

_____

_____

_____

Notes

## 5 | Getting further — Extension

### Task repetition

1. Now, get a different picture from the teacher. This time, write down *only four words* that you need to describe your picture, but you don't know in English.

_____  _____  _____  _____

2. Work with your partner and find the differences. This time, you don't know how many differences there are. Keep talking and find as many differences as possible.

## 6 | Getting it done — Wrap up

### Write about differences

Write six sentences that explain some of the differences in the second set of pictures.

1. _____

2. _____

3. _____

4. _____

5. _____

6. _____

Attach your picture here.

## Unit 5 | Put a name to the desk

**Goal** To identify the owners of the desks
机の所有者を当てる

### 1 | Getting warmed up

**Describe the person**

| | | | |
|---|---|---|---|
| Natalie | Ella | Mia | Grace |
| Emily | Aubrey | Mary | Linda |
| Carol | Ava | Sophia | Amelia |

---

**PART A**

Work in a pair.

**Student A :** Choose a person from the pictures above.

**Student B :** Guess which person your partner chose by asking questions. Your questions must have 'yes/no' answers.

Swap roles and do it again. The person who guesses correctly with the fewest questions is the winner.

Number of questions I asked: ☐    Number of questions my partner asked: ☐

---

**PART B**

Look again at the picture of the person you chose in PART A, and imagine her character and personality. If you opened the drawer of that person's work desk, what do you think you would see inside? Write your ideas in the space.

Person's name: _____

Things I might see inside her desk:

## 2 | Getting ready

### Vocabulary building

Consider the pictures of the desks, and imagine the character/personality of the desk owner. For example, is the owner of the desk young or old? Are they male or female? What are their hobbies or interests? Are they shy, outgoing, serious or easy-going? Write your ideas on the lines below.

Attach your sheet here.

## 3 | Getting into it

### Guess the owner of the desk

Work in a pair. Student A looks at Sheet B1, and Student B gets Sheet B2 from the teacher. There are descriptions of four different teachers on each sheet. The goal of this task is to match the desks with the teachers.

PREPARATION

Read the descriptions of the teachers and write some keywords in the space below to help you discuss them.

_____

_____

_____

_____

_____

_____

_____

_____

DISCUSSION

Turn your sheet over so that you cannot see it. Together, look at the pictures of the desks and use your notes above to discuss the teachers and the desks, and try to match them together. Write your guesses in the table below.

| A | | B | | C | | D | | E | | F | | G | | H | |
|---|---|---|---|---|---|---|---|---|---|---|---|---|---|---|---|

## 4 | Getting better at it — Language focus

### Reflection

What are some words or expressions in English that were useful to complete this task?

_____

_____

_____

_____

What are some words or expressions in Japanese that you wanted to use, but couldn't?

_____

_____

_____

_____

Notes

## 5 | Getting further  — Extension

**Listen to a description of your teacher's desk**

The teacher will describe his/her desk. Listen carefully. Use the space below to draw a picture of your teacher's desk. If you don't want to draw a picture, you can take notes instead.

## 6 | Getting it done  — Wrap up

**Write a profile based on the desk**

Write a profile of your teacher's character, based upon the description of the desk above and your knowledge of your teacher.

# 6 Get your story straight

**Goal**  To find the differences between two stories
２つの物語の間の違いを指摘する

## 1 Getting warmed up

**Guess the title**

1. Write the titles of these well-known stories.

**A. Title:** _____

One little pig built a house of straw, but a wolf came and destroyed the house. His brother built a house of sticks, but the wolf destroyed that, too. So, the pigs took shelter in the third brother's house, which was made from bricks.

**B. Title:** _____

While a young boy was away from his home, demons came and attacked his family. His sister survived, but she was changed into a demon. He then devoted himself to finding a way to change her back into a human.

**C. Title:** _____

A young boy's parents were killed, so he was brought up by his cruel uncle and aunt. Gradually, he discovered that he possesses magical powers. He escaped from his uncle and aunt and went to a boarding school to develop his power.

**D. Title:** _____

In ancient Japan, a man is fired from his job as a servant. Having no money, he contemplated whether it is better to starve to death or to become a thief. He met an old woman who was stealing hair from dead bodies, and he brutally robbed her of her clothes.

2. Write some notes to help you tell a short summary of a well-known story to your group. Your group will guess the title. It can be a story from a book, a comic, a film or a TV show.

## 2 Getting ready

**The same story told differently**

Work in a pair.
Compare these two stories of *The Hare and the Tortoise.*

**Story A**

A long time ago, there lived a hare who always boasted of his running speed. He would often tease the tortoise for being the slowest animal around. One fine day, he dared the tortoise to a race in order to show off his skills in front of the other animals in the forest. Fed up with the hare's bragging, the tortoise accepted the challenge.

On the day of the race, all the animals of the forest gathered to watch the competition between the hare and the tortoise. Just as they were about to begin the race, the hare mocked the tortoise for accepting the challenge. The tortoise ignored the hare's words and kept silent.

The race began, and soon the tortoise was left far behind. The hare decided to take a short nap so that he would further humiliate the tortoise.

Soon the hare fell into a deep sleep. To his dismay, when he woke up the tortoise was just a few steps away from the finish line. The hare rushed towards it as fast as he could, but it was too late and the tortoise crossed the finish line, thereby winning the competition.

When the hare reached the point where the race ended, all the animals were laughing at him for losing the race to the tortoise.

**Story B**

There once was a speedy hare who always bragged about how fast he could run. "Ha ha! I'm the fastest animal in the forest! No one can beat me!" he would often cry. Tired of hearing him boast, the tortoise challenged him to a race. All the animals in the forest gathered to watch.

The owl called the start of the race. "Ready, set, go!" he shouted.

The hare took off and ran down the road as fast as lightning. After a while, he paused to rest. He looked back at the tortoise and saw how far he was behind. "I'm going to win easily," he thought. "That tortoise is so slow!"

The hare wanted to look fit and fresh when he won the race, so he laid down in the grass for a moment. "There is plenty of time to relax," he thought as he fell asleep.

The tortoise walked on and on, never ever stopping until he crossed the finish line. The animals who were watching cheered so loudly for the tortoise that they woke up the hare. The hare stretched, yawned and began to run again, but it was too late. The tortoise had already won the race.

Moral: Slow and steady wins the race.

Check the correct box. Which story...                                    Story A     Story B

a. mentions a third animal, apart from the hare and the tortoise?      ☐           ☐

b. has more direct quotes from the animals?                            ☐           ☐

c. explains the morality lesson to be learned?                         ☐           ☐

d. emphasises the mean attitude of the hare towards the tortoise?      ☐           ☐

e. is aimed at a younger audience?                                     ☐           ☐

## 3 Getting into it

### Compare two stories

Work in a pair. You will get a story handout from your teacher and your partner will get the same story, told differently. Your task is to find the differences in the stories.

1. Read your story, and take some notes of the main points below.

_____

_____

_____

_____

_____

_____

2. Use your notes to retell the story to your partner. Listen to your partner's story, and together note down the differences. There may be differences in the facts of the story (the action), and there may also be differences in the style of the story (the way it is written).

*Differences between Story A and Story B.*

| STORY A | STORY B |
|---------|---------|
|         |         |
|         |         |
|         |         |
|         |         |

## 4 Getting better at it   *Language focus*

### Reflection

What are some words or expressions in English that were useful to complete this task?

_____

_____

_____

What are some words or expressions in Japanese that you wanted to use, but couldn't?

_____

_____

_____

Notes

## 5 | Getting further   ⟨ *Extension* ⟩

### Tell a story

As a class, choose a story that everyone knows.

1. Half the class (Group A) will tell the story one way, and the other half of the class (Group B) will tell the same story differently. Work with a partner in your group. Do not write the complete story, but take some notes to help you tell the story orally.

| *Group A story* | *Group B story* |
| --- | --- |
| • aimed at younger children<br>• has action and suspense<br>• does not have much dialogue | • aimed at older children<br>• has romance<br>• has a lot of dialogue |

*Story notes:*

2. Find a partner from the other group. Tell each other your stories. Make some notes below about the main differences in your partner's story.

*Main points of difference in partner's story:*

## 6 | Getting it done   ⟨ *Wrap up* ⟩

### Write your story

Use your notes from 5 **Getting further** to write your story on a separate piece of paper.

Attach your sheet here.

# Lie through your teeth

**Goal** To interrogate a person in order to spot a lie
嘘を見破るために相手を質問攻めにする

## 1 | Getting warmed up

**Match the questions and answers**

1. Match each question with an answer.

| | |
|---|---|
| 1. What did you do last weekend? | a) I took the train in the morning and arrived about 10:30. |
| 2. How did you get there? | b) Well, I forgot to bring my student ID card, so I had to pay the adult price. |
| 3. What was the exhibition? | c) I'm not sure, really. They were all pretty good. |
| 4. How much did it cost? | d) I went and saw an exhibition at the City Museum. |
| 5. Which painting did you like the most? | e) I arrived late in the evening because I got caught in a traffic jam. |
| 6. What time did you get home? | f) It was a collection of modern paintings from New York. |

2. One of these answers is a lie. Which one do you think it is?

## 2 | Getting ready

**Prepare your answers**

1. The teacher will give you a question or a topic.

   Write it here: _____

2. Prepare three answers. One of your answers is a lie, and the other two answers are true. Note as much detail in your answers as you can: what, why, when, how, who, etc. You should make your answers convincing, so that your group members cannot spot the lie.

| Answer 1 | Answer 2 | Answer 3 |
|---|---|---|
| | | |
| | | |
| | | |
| | | |

## 3 | Getting into it

### Spot the lie

Work in a group. Listen to your group members' answers, and ask as many questions as you can to spot the lie.

## 4 | Getting better at it    Language focus

### Reflection

| | |
|---|---|
| What are some words or expressions in English that were useful to complete this task? | What are some words or expressions in Japanese that you wanted to use, but couldn't? |

Notes

## 5 | Getting further    Extension

### Task repetition

Change groups. Do the task again with a different question/topic.

Write it here: _____

| Answer 1 | Answer 2 | Answer 3 |
|---|---|---|
| | | |

## 6 | Getting it done    Wrap up

### Write an unbelievable story

Choose one of your lies from this lesson. On a separate piece of paper, write a detailed story and make it as fantastic or as unbelievable as you can.

## Unit 8 — After the quake

**Goal** To predict how a room will change
屋内の状況の変化を予測する

### 1 Getting warmed up

**List the objects in a room**

Imagine a typical Japanese house with an open plan design (i.e., the living room, the dining room and the kitchen are all in the same space). What decorations and objects and other things might you see in the room? List as many as possible. If you don't know the English word, you can write it in Japanese, and then look it up.

### 2 Getting ready

**Challenge your memory**

1. Work in a pair. Each pair gets a picture from the teacher. Together, look very carefully at each thing in the picture and try to memorize what you see. After 30 seconds, turn the picture over.
2. The teacher will say six sentences about the picture. Is each sentence true or false? Without looking at the picture, but only relying on your memory, choose either true (T) or false (F).

   1. T / F    2. T / F    3. T / F    4. T / F    5. T / F    6. T / F

3. Turn the paper back over and look at the picture again to check your answers.

*The main task!*

### 3 Getting into it

**Guess the changes**

PART A

Work in a pair. Student A keeps the picture used in 2 **Getting ready** (Picture 1), and Student B gets a new picture from the teacher (Picture 2). This picture is of the same room, with the same people and the same objects, after a level 5 earthquake has struck.

**Student A :** Look at Picture 1 and guess what is happening in Picture 2. Tell your ideas to your partner, giving as much detail as you can.

**Student B :** Listen to your partner, while looking at Picture 2, and check if your partner's guesses are accurate. Continue until your partner makes 10 correct guesses. Take some short notes (below) of the 10 guesses that your partner gets correct. Be quick. Show your notes to the teacher to get Picture 3.

1. _____
2. _____
3. _____
4. _____
5. _____
6. _____
7. _____
8. _____
9. _____
10. _____

---

### PART B

The teacher will give Picture 3 to Student A. This is the same room again, after a level 6 earthquake has struck. Repeat the same steps as in PART A, with Student B guessing how the room has changed. Student A takes quick notes below.

1. _____
2. _____
3. _____
4. _____
5. _____
6. _____
7. _____
8. _____
9. _____
10. _____

Attach your picture here.

## 4 │ Getting better at it  〈 Language focus 〉

### Reflection

What are some words or expressions in English that were useful to complete this task?

_____

_____

_____

_____

What are some words or expressions in Japanese that you wanted to use, but couldn't?

_____

_____

_____

_____

Notes

## 5 │ Getting further  〈 Extension 〉

### Guess what happens next

1. Try and guess how the situation would change after a much stronger, level 7 earthquake.
2. The teacher will show you a picture of the house after a level 7 earthquake. Were your guesses correct? How could you describe the condition of the house in the picture? Take notes of your ideas in the space below.

Notes

## 6 | Getting it done   Wrap up

**Prepare for an earthquake**

You have probably heard people tell you what to do to prepare a room so that it is safe in an earthquake. Look at Picture 3 again. In order to prevent this happening in the room, what should the family have done before the earthquake came? Write down five ideas so that you can share them in the class. (Creative ideas are welcome!)

1. _____

2. _____

3. _____

4. _____

5. _____

Attach your picture here.

## Unit 9 | Search for something in common

**Goal** To find something in common with other people
他の人との共通点を見つける

### 1 | Getting warmed up

**Learn about your teacher**

1. The teacher will tell you about his/her interests, hobbies, talents, habits, values, likes and dislikes, past experiences, dreams for the future, and so on. Listen carefully, and make a note below of all the things that are similar to yourself.

1. _____     2. _____

3. _____     4. _____

5. _____     6. _____

2. See how many people have something in common with the teacher, following his/her instructions.

### 2 | Getting ready

**Describe yourself**

Now, think about yourself. Look at the categories below and write as many keywords as you can for each one. You can write more than one thing for each category. Only write those things which you are comfortable telling your classmates.

| Background and experience | |
| --- | --- |
| Interests | |
| Likes and dislikes | |
| Personality | |
| Knowledge and special abilities/skills | |
| Lifestyle | |
| Beliefs and ambitions | |
| Important events in life | |
| Other | |

## 3 Getting into it

### Find things in common with your group

Work in a group. Choose one person to be the discussion leader. The goal of the discussion is to find things in common with the people in your group. Find as many things as you can.

Each person will talk about himself/herself. Listen to them. As soon as you hear something that is the same for you, tell your group. You can ask questions to get more information. Note down all the things that two or more people in your group have in common. You will be asked to give a report of your findings later.

| Names | Things in common |
|---|---|
|  |  |
|  |  |
|  |  |
|  |  |
|  |  |
|  |  |
|  |  |
|  |  |
|  |  |
|  |  |
|  |  |
|  |  |
|  |  |
|  |  |
|  |  |
|  |  |
|  |  |
|  |  |
|  |  |
|  |  |

## 4 | Getting better at it Language focus

### Reflection

What are some words or expressions in English that were useful to complete this task?

_____

_____

_____

_____

What are some words or expressions in Japanese that you wanted to use, but couldn't?

_____

_____

_____

_____

Notes

## 5 | Getting further Extension

### Task repetition

To get to know about more of your classmates, do the task again with a new group. Based on your experience doing the task the first time, try and make your discussion go even more smoothly, and make even more interesting discoveries about the people in your group.

| Names | Things in common |
|-------|------------------|
|       |                  |
|       |                  |
|       |                  |
|       |                  |
|       |                  |
|       |                  |
|       |                  |
|       |                  |
|       |                  |

|  |  |
|---|---|
|  |  |
|  |  |
|  |  |
|  |  |
|  |  |
|  |  |
|  |  |

## 6 Getting it done  ⟨ Wrap up ⟩

### Write a report

Look at the notes you made for both the first and second group. Choose the four most interesting or surprising things that people had in common and write a report.

**Goal** To put the pictures in order
絵を正しい順番に並べる

## 1 Getting warmed up

**Put the pictures in order**

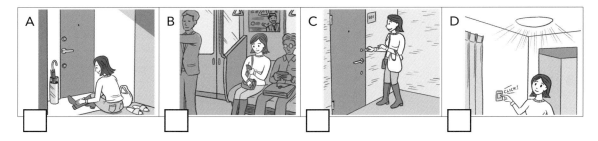

Work in a pair. Speak with your partner. What is happening in each picture? Put the story in order. Number the pictures 1 ~ 4.

## 2 Getting ready

**Match the descriptions to the pictures**

Work in a pair. Read the instructions on how to make gratin and match the statements to the pictures.

A: Boil the macaroni in plenty of water. Slice the bacon and the onion into thin strips and cut the chicken into bite-size pieces.

B: Pour the heated milk into the pot with the flour and butter. Whisk it all together and add some salt and pepper.

C: Grease the inside of an oven dish with butter and then pour in the mixture. Sprinkle some cheese on top and then bake in a preheated oven at 250 degrees for 12 minutes.

D: Fry the onion, bacon and chicken in a frying pan. Add some white wine and fry some more.

E: Add the cooked macaroni and the white sauce to the mixture in the frying pan and stir everything together.

F: Put some butter in a saucepan and then add flour. Heat it and stir to make a white sauce.

## 3 | Getting into it

### Put the recipe in the correct order

Work in a pair. Each student gets a handout from the teacher.

Your task is to put a recipe for chicken pot pie into the correct order. There are ten steps in the recipe, and each student has five steps. *Do not look at your partner's paper.* Speak together, figure out the order of the recipe, and then write it in the table below.

| 1 | 2 | 3 | 4 | 5 | 6 | 7 | 8 | 9 | 10 |
|---|---|---|---|---|---|---|---|---|----|
|   |   |   |   |   |   |   |   |   |    |

## 4 | Getting better at it  Language focus

### Reflection

What are some words or expressions in English that were useful to complete this task?

_____

_____

_____

_____

What are some words or expressions in Japanese that you wanted to use, but couldn't?

_____

_____

_____

_____

Notes

Attach your picture here.

## 5 | Getting further ⟨ *Extension* ⟩

**Watch a video on how to make a chicken pot pie**

Work in a pair. You will watch a video that explains how to make a chicken pot pie.

*Student A :* Explain the steps in the recipe as you watch the video, giving as much detail as possible.

*Student B :* Listen carefully to your partner's explanation and compare it with your recipe sequence in 3 **Getting into it**. Are there any differences? Write the differences in the space below.

## 6 Getting it done — Wrap up

### Write your own recipe

Write a recipe for your favourite meal or snack. Give as much detail as possible.

# Life in a train carriage

**Goal** To put the pictures in order
絵を正しい順に並べる

## 1 Getting warmed up

**Listen and draw**

1. Your teacher is going to describe three people to add to the picture below. Listen carefully and draw them in their proper places.

2. Compare your answers with a partner.

## 2 Getting ready

**Vocabulary building**

1. Get a worksheet from your teacher. Are there any actions or situations you don't know how to describe in English? Write them in Japanese in the space below.
2. Speak with a classmate who has the same worksheet as you and compare your lists. Think together about how you can express the actions or situations in English.

## 3 | Getting into it

### Put the pictures in order

Work with a partner who has a different worksheet to you. Put the pictures in order *without looking at your partner's worksheet.*

## 4 | Getting better at it    Language focus

### Reflection

What are some words or expressions in English that were useful to complete this task?

What are some words or expressions in Japanese that you wanted to use, but couldn't?

Notes

Attach your picture here.

## 5 | Getting further    Extension

### Guess what happens next

Work in a pair. Look at the final picture. In the next scene, the old lady gets a big shock. What do you think it could be? Think of three possibilities. Then, share your ideas with the class.

- 
- 
- 

## 6 | Getting it done    Wrap up

### Write a story

Describe the whole story, including the final scene you created with your partner.

## Unit 12 — The suspicious mother

**Goal** To tell a story in a logical order
ストーリーの断片を正しい順に並べる

### 1 | Getting warmed up

**Discuss the title**

You will read a story in this unit. Here is the title:

> MOM SUSPECTED HER SON OF SLEEPING WITH HIS ROOMMATE. WHAT SHE DID NEXT WAS PERFECT.

Work in a pair. Check what the following expressions mean:
- suspect _____
- 'perfect' in WHAT SHE DID NEXT WAS PERFECT _____

### 2 | Getting ready

**Predict the story**

1. Read the beginning of the story.

   > A mom visited her son for dinner who was sharing a house with a girl. During the meal, his mother couldn't help but notice how pretty his roommate was. She had long suspected they were having a romantic relationship and this only made her more suspicious.

2. Work in a pair. Imagine that you are the mom. What questions would you ask your son and his roommate? Remember that you love your son and you do not want to embarrass him in front of his roommate, and you do not want to be rude to his roommate either, but you are VERY curious about their relationship. Write your questions below.

   _____

   _____

   _____

3. Share your questions with the class.

4. What does 'this' mean in the third sentence, "...this only made her more suspicious?" Write your answer below.

   _____

   _____

5. Share your answer with the class.

## 3 | Getting into it

### Decide a logical order

You will read the rest of the story. However, the lines are jumbled up. Put them in order.

*Do not look at your partner's paper.* The first sentence of the story is in Sheet A, and it is marked. If you put the lines in the correct order, the story will be completed.

When you finish, work with your partner and write a summary of the story in one or two sentences.

## 4 | Getting better at it

### Reflection

What are some words or expressions in English that were useful to complete this task?

What are some words or expressions in Japanese that you wanted to use, but couldn't?

> Notes

## 5 | Getting further

### Write an email

Imagine you are the son. Write an email to respond to your mother. Write 80-100 words.

## 6 | Getting it done

### Write a reply

Read the email your partner wrote. Imagine you are the mother. Read the email from your son and write a reply. Write 80-100 words.

Attach your sheet here.

# Unit 13 | Catch the criminal

**Goal** To read the details of a crime and guess the criminal

与えられた情報から犯人を推測する

## 1 | Getting warmed up

### Vocabulary building

Read the following definitions. What word is being described? The first letter is given.

1. To roughly calculate the number (verb)      e _____

2. A person who was injured or killed as a result of a crime or an accident (noun)      v _____

3. To kill someone (verb)      m _____

4. Planned for at a certain time (adjective)      d _____ to

5. A person thought to be guilty of a crime or offence (noun)      s _____

6. A thing that you buy and/or keep to remind yourself of a place, an occasion or a holiday (noun)      s _____

## 2 | Getting ready

### Understand the outline of the story

Imagine that you are a police detective. Your task is to find the criminal.

1. First, read the Police Report provided by the Police Chief.

> • On July 3rd, in the village of Southgate, a man was murdered.
> • The victim was a security guard at Southgate High School.
> • The victim's name is Harry (male, 36).
> • The estimated time of death is between 7:00 p.m. and 7:30 p.m.
> • On the day of the murder, the victim was working the afternoon shift and was due to finish at 7:15 p.m.
> • The victim's body was found on the floor of the security guards' office.
> • On the floor near the body was a chocolate box and a number of chocolates.
> • Poison was discovered on the victim's fingers, the chocolate box, and the inside and outside knobs of the security guards' office door.
> • There was no poison found on the chocolates.

2. Work in a pair. Draw a picture of the crime scene. Write important words and numbers in the picture.

### 3 Getting into it

**Examine the details**

1. Work in a group of four. Together, you are the investigative team. You will get a Suspect Card that describes one of the four suspects. Each member will get a different Suspect Card.
2. Read the Suspect Card in five minutes. Try to remember as much information as possible and take notes below.
3. After five minutes, return the card to your teacher.
4. Explain what was written on your Suspect Card to your group members.

| Notes on your suspect | Notes on other students' suspects |
| --- | --- |
| | |

5. Talk together and work out who the criminal is. Then, share your answers with the class.

**4 Getting better at it** — *Language focus*

### Reflection

What are some words or expressions in English that were useful to complete this task?

What are some words or expressions in Japanese that you wanted to use, but couldn't?

Notes

**5 Getting further** — *Extension*

### Piece together the crime

Make a timeline of the events in the story. Include the following information:
- What each person in the story did
- Where and when each event took place

## Write a report

Write an investigation report to the Police Chief explaining in detail how the crime was committed.

# Unit 14 | Storytelling with cartoons

**Goal** To tell a story with a cartoon
一連の絵で表現されたストーリーの展開を説明する

## 1 | Getting warmed up

### Vocabulary building

Work in a pair. Decide who is the storyteller and who is the listener. The storyteller gets a picture story from the teacher. *Do not show your pictures to your partner.*

**Storyteller :** Look at your pictures and make a list of words in Japanese that you will need to explain the story. Write the words in the table and tell your partner.

**Listener :** Write the Japanese words in the table and then look them up in English. Write the English translation, and tell your partner.

| Japanese | English |
|---|---|
|  |  |
|  |  |
|  |  |
|  |  |
|  |  |
|  |  |

## 2 | Getting ready

### Make up a story

**Listener :** Look at your list of words (above) and use them to create an original story. Your story should have six sentences. Use the sentence starters below to tell the story to your partner.

| | |
|---|---|
| 1. One day... | 4. After that... |
| 2. Then... | 5. Fortunately... |
| 3. Suddenly... | 6. In the end... |

**Storyteller :** Listen to your partner's story and evaluate how interesting it is.

## 3 Getting into it

### Storytelling

PART A

*Storyteller :* Look at your pictures from 1 **Getting warmed up** and tell the story to your partner. Tell your partner each stage of the story (a~j) so that they can hear all the main points. Give as much detail as possible.

*Listener :* Don't look at the pictures, but listen to the story. Take some notes or draw some rough pictures in the boxes below (a~j) to help you remember it. (You will repeat the main points of the story to your partner later.)

| a | b |
|---|---|
| c | d |
| e | f |
| g | h |
| i | j |

PART B

*Listener :* Look back at your notes and repeat each part of the story to your partner. If your partner says it is correct, put a check ✔ in the box.

*Storyteller :* Listen to each point and say if it is correct or not. If it is incorrect, explain the reason.

PART C

Together in your pair, write the complete story. You can both look at the pictures now.

Attach your picture here.

## 4 Getting better at it ⟨ *Language focus* ⟩

### Reflection

What are some words or expressions in English that were useful to complete this task?

_____

_____

_____

_____

What are some words or expressions in Japanese that you wanted to use, but couldn't?

_____

_____

_____

_____

Notes

## 5 Getting further ⟨ *Extension* ⟩

### Task repetition

With the same partner, swap roles, and the new storyteller gets a different picture story from the teacher. *Do not show your pictures to your partner.*

**Storyteller :** Look at your pictures and make a list of words in Japanese that you will need to explain the story. Write the words in the table and tell your partner.

**Listener :** Write the Japanese words in the table and then look them up in English. Write the English translation, and tell your partner.

| Japanese | English |
|---|---|
| | |
| | |
| | |
| | |
| | |
| | |

***Storyteller :*** Look at your pictures and tell the story to your partner. Tell your partner each stage of the story (a~f) so that they can get all the main points.

***Listener :*** Don't look at the pictures, but listen to the story. Take some notes or draw some rough pictures in the boxes below (a~f) to help you remember it. (You will repeat the main points of the story to your partner later.)

| a ☐ | b ☐ |
|---|---|
| c ☐ | d ☐ |
| e ☐ | f ☐ |

**PART B**

***Listener :*** Look back at your notes and repeat each part of the story to your partner. If your partner says it is correct, put a check ✔ in the box.

***Storyteller :*** Listen to each point and say if it is correct or not. If it is incorrect, explain the reason.

## 6 | Getting it done 〈 Wrap up 〉

### Writing

Write the complete story in 5 **Getting further**, giving as much detail as you can.

**Goal** To describe an event as it is happening
出来事をその展開と同時進行で人に説明していく

## 1 | Getting warmed up

**Watch a story from a TV commercial**

1. Watch the short TV commercial *English for Beginners*. Close this book. Don't take any notes while you are watching, and try to remember as much as you can.

2. Look at the descriptions of some scenes in the story. Some of the descriptions are false. Based on what you remember, correct the false descriptions so that they are true.

   a. An elderly man is working on a computer.

   b. He is unwrapping a book called 'English for Beginners'.

   c. He is reading the book on a bus.

   d. He is taking a bath and practicing speaking to a toy whale.

   e. He is packing his slippers and a toothbrush into a suitcase.

   f. His dog is going to the airport with him.

   g. The man is taking a train to someone's house at nighttime.

   h. A little girl is coming out of her room to see the man.

## 2 | Getting ready

**Think about the characters and the situation**

Work in a pair. You will watch another short story. Firstly, you will see only the opening part. What words and expressions can you use to describe what you see? Think about the people and the animals, the place, the objects and action. Discuss it with your partner and the teacher, and write notes in the space on the next page.
Here are some important details to help you:

- The main character (a sheep) is called **Shaun**.
- The place is called **a farm**.
- The owner of the farm is known as **The Farmer**.
- The dog's name is **Bitzer**.
- The house for the animals is called **a barn**.

Notes

## 3 | Getting into it

### Tell the story

PART A

Work in a pair. The teacher will play the first two minutes of the episode *Shaun the Fugitive*.

***Student A :*** Sit with your chair facing the front, so that you can see the screen. As you watch, explain what is happening to your partner.

***Student B :*** Turn your chair around and face the back of the room, so that you *cannot* see the screen. Listen to your partner's explanation and imagine the story.

The teacher will pause the video for a while. During the time, Student A can add any extra information to explain the story, and Student B can ask questions about the points that they didn't understand. Use the space below to make notes.

Notes

PART B

Switch roles. Student A face the back of the room, and Student B face the screen.

The next two minutes of the story will be shown. Student B, explain the story to your partner as you watch.

When the teacher pauses the video after two minutes, speak together and confirm what happened, asking questions and adding any extra information. Use the space on the next page to note keywords.

PART C

Watch the entire first four minutes of the story again, all together. Check that you understood the story correctly.

## 4 Getting better at it — Language focus

### Reflection

What are some words or expressions in English that were useful to complete this task?

_____

_____

_____

_____

What are some words or expressions in Japanese that you wanted to use, but couldn't?

_____

_____

_____

_____

Notes

## 5 Getting further — Extension

### Predict the ending

1. There are two minutes remaining in the story. How will it end? What do you think will happen? Predict the end of the story with your partner.

Notes

2. After listening to the ideas by other pairs, watch the final part of the story to see whose predictions were correct.

## 6 | Getting it done ⟨Wrap up⟩

### Write the story

Write the complete story, from beginning to end, so that someone who has never seen this episode can understand it. Make sure you include all the main points, giving details when necessary. You may use your smartphone or other device to watch the video as many times as you need.

# Figure out the puzzle

**Goal** To use your creative problem-solving skills to find the solution to some puzzles

論理性や発想の柔軟さを発揮してクイズの答えを考える

## 1 | Getting warmed up

**Find the odd one out**

1. There are four words in each group. One word is different to the rest for some reason. Circle the odd one out and write the reason.

| | *Circle the odd one out* | | | | *Reason* |
|---|---|---|---|---|---|
| *e.g.* | Spanish | (Hungarian) | Italian | French | *Hungarian is the only language not derived from Latin.* |
| 1 | Paris | Tokyo | Sydney | Ottawa | |
| 2 | buy | cry | sigh | bury | |
| 3 | earns | rinse | risen | siren | |
| 4 | turnip | carrot | cauliflower | radish | |

2. Compare your ideas with those of other students. Revise your answer if you find another idea more plausible. The teacher will provide you with the answers after you have reached a conclusion.

## 2 │ Getting ready

### Work it out

You will receive a handout from your teacher which has five logic puzzles on it. Try and solve as many puzzles as you can in the time limit, starting with any question you would like. You don't have to solve them all. Also, if you only solve part of a puzzle, that's OK too. Use the space below to take notes of your ideas.

Attach your sheet here.

## 3 │ Getting into it

### Discuss the solutions

1. Work in a pair or a group of three. Use your notes (above) to discuss your ideas about the puzzles. Together, try and find a solution to as many of the puzzles as you can. Use the space below to take notes of your ideas.

2. Join with another pair or a group. Pool your ideas together and try to find solutions to more of the puzzles. Use the space below to take notes of your ideas.

3. Share your ideas with the whole class.

## 4 | Getting better at it  — Language focus

### Reflection

What are some words or expressions in English that were useful to complete this task?

What are some words or expressions in Japanese that you wanted to use, but couldn't?

Notes

## 5 | Getting further  — Extension

### Check the solutions

The teacher will give you a handout with the solutions to the puzzles. Check these solutions with your group's solutions and see if there is any match. See how many solutions other groups were able to find?

## 6 | Getting it done  — Wrap up

### Write a puzzle

Think of a fun problem that you know. On a separate piece of paper, write the problem and the solution in English. You may write any kind of problem, such as a logic puzzle, a riddle, or a quiz.

**Unit 17** **Figure out the relationships**

**Goal** To read the story and figure out the relationships

物語を読み、人間関係を把握する

## 1 | Getting warmed up

**Draw a family tree**

Read the following passage and complete the family tree diagram with the correct names.

Abby has two sons and two daughters. Her youngest daughter Amy is single. Abby also has four grandchildren. Her granddaughters' names are Shelly and Tarah. Amy's siblings are Marty, Sarah and Alan. Marty's father is Carlyle. Marty has two sons.

Trent's wife is called Sarah. Posy is Marty's wife, and they have a son named Rod. Rod's brother is called John. Rachel is married but she doesn't have any kids. Trent's father-in-law is Carlyle.

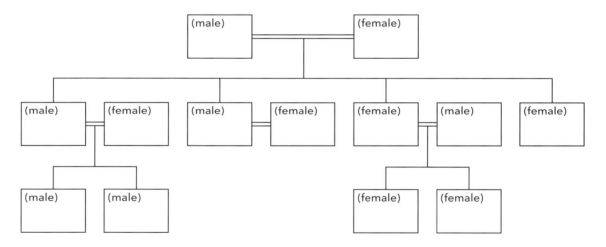

## 2 | Getting ready

**Vocabulary building**

音声ページ ⑴

1. Listen to the audio of a story. Write down any words you don't know or details that you can't understand. Write your notes in the space below.
2. Compare your notes with a partner.
3. Listen again, and try to understand some more of the story.
4. Read the story on page 65 together, and add to your notes.

Notes

## 3 | Getting into it

**Figure out the relationships**

1. Work in a pair. Look again at the story on page 65. Based upon the story, try to complete the diagram of character relationships.

2. Join with another pair to make a group. Share your ideas, and together create one answer that you all think is correct.

## 4 | Getting better at it — Language focus

**Reflection**

What are some words or expressions in English that were useful to complete this task?

What are some words or expressions in Japanese that you wanted to use, but couldn't?

Notes

## 5 | Getting further — Extension

**Make up a story**

1. Work in a pair or in a group. The story can be divided into three parts: the beginning, the middle, and the end. The story on page 65 is only the middle part. Imagine what happened before and what happened after, and create an original story.

   Each group will report their story to the class, so also decide who the reporter will be.

| |
|---|
| *What happened before:* |
| *What happened after:* |

2. Each pair or group tells the class their story.
3. Take a vote on which story you think is the best.

The pair or group with the best story: _____

Reason: _____

## 6 Getting it done  ⟨ Wrap up ⟩

音声ページ  Beginning 02  End 03

### Write the plot

1. Listen to the actual beginning and end of the story from the original text. Afterwards, you will write a summary of the plot, so take some notes of the story as you listen.
2. Write a summary of the plot from the original text.

Notes

*Plot summary*

_____

_____

_____

_____

_____

_____

This rather aggressive regard for privacy reminds me very much of her sister. For in truth, my two daughters had much in common, much more than my husband would ever admit. As far as he was concerned, they were complete opposites; furthermore, it became his view that Keiko was a difficult person by nature and there was little we could do for her. In fact, although he never claimed it outright, he would imply that Keiko inherited her personality from her father. I did little to contradict this, for it was the easy explanation, that Jiro was to blame, not us. Of course, my husband never knew Keiko in her early years; if he had, he may well have recognized how similar the two girls were during their respective early stages. Both had fierce tempers, both were possessive; if they became upset, they would not forget their anger quickly like other children, but would remain moody for most of the day. And yet, one has become a happy, confident young woman — I have every hope for Niki's future — while the other, after becoming increasingly miserable, took her own life. I do not find it as easy as my husband did to put the blame on Nature, or else on Jiro. However, such things are in the past now, and there is little to be gained in going over them here.

**The Relationships among the Characters**

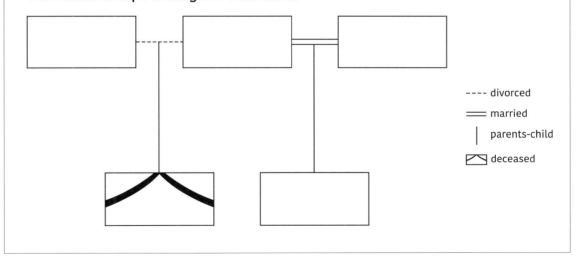

---- divorced

══ married

| parents-child

◁▷ deceased

Audio files for a different story.

 音声ページ

 Story 04

 Beginning 05

 End 06

# Origami challenge

**Goal** To create art together by following instructions
指示に従い協力してモノを創作する

## 1  Getting warmed up

**Guess the vocabulary**

1. Work in a pair. In this lesson, you're going to read and listen to instructions on how to make some origami. Guess what vocabulary might be used in the instructions. Write down as many words and phrases as possible in the space below.

2. Compare your vocabulary list with another pair. Add any extra words the other pair wrote.

## 2  Getting ready

**Check your guesses**

Get an instruction sheet from your teacher. Read the instructions and circle the words that are in your vocabulary list in **1 Getting warmed up**. How many words did you guess correctly?

**The number of successfully guessed words:** _____

## 3  Getting into it

**Make some origami**

Get a piece of origami paper from your teacher. With your partner, follow the instructions and make the origami. While you work with your partner, speak in English as much as possible.

## 4  Getting better at it  ⟨ Language focus ⟩

**Reflection**

What are some useful words or expressions in English that you used during this task?

What are some words or expressions in Japanese that you wanted to use, but you didn't know the English?

Notes

## 5 | Getting further ⟨ *Extension* ⟩

### Task repetition

Get another piece of origami paper from your teacher. This time, you're going to follow audio instructions. With your partner, listen to the instructions and make the origami.

Instruction A  (07)     Instruction B (08)     Instruction C (09)

音声ページ

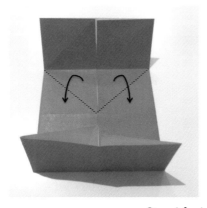 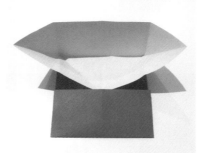

Step 6 for Instruction C

## 6 | Getting it done ⟨ *Wrap up* ⟩

### Give advice

If your friends are going to make origami by reading or listening to instructions, what advice would you give to them? Think about what was difficult for you and how to overcome the difficulty. Write some advice below.

Attach your origami here.

# Unit 19 | Japanese life satisfaction

**Goal** To compare two texts on the same topic
同じトピックについて書かれた2つの文章を比較する

## 1 Getting warmed up

**Guess the countries**

1. Look at the figure below. This is part of the results of a survey that investigated young people's beliefs about themselves and society. The missing countries are US, Sweden, and Japan. With your partner, guess which country names go in the blanks. Then, write the reasons for your guesses.

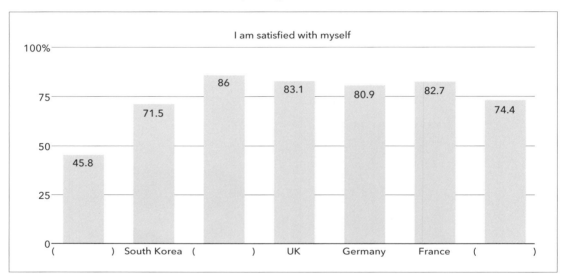

Note. The percentage of young people who chose "I agree" or "I kind of agree" in response the statement "I am satisfied with myself". Taken from White Paper on Children and Young People 2014.

*Reasons*

2. Here are three statements from the survey. Do you agree? Put a check in the box below and then compare your answers with your partner.

|  | I agree | I kind of agree | I don't agree | I really don't agree |
|---|---|---|---|---|
| I am satisfied with myself. | ☐ | ☐ | ☐ | ☐ |
| I am hopeful about the future. | ☐ | ☐ | ☐ | ☐ |
| I expect to be happy when I am 40 years old. | ☐ | ☐ | ☐ | ☐ |

## 2 | Getting ready

### Interpret the figure

What can you tell from the figure shown on the left page? Talk to your partner and interpret the data below.

## 3 | Getting into it

### Compare two texts

Imagine that you're working at a TV station. Your daily task is to read some news articles, to summarize them, and to report to your boss.

1. First, read the following two articles that report on the findings of research into attitudes of young people today.

---

**Young Japanese least hopeful for the future**

Young people in Japan are the least hopeful about their future among seven surveyed countries, a government white paper has revealed.

In the survey, featured in the 2014 Children and Youth White Paper, 61.6 percent of Japanese respondents answered that they have hope or a degree of hope for their future, much lower than 82.4 percent to 91.1 percent in the other six countries—South Korea, the United States, Britain, Germany, France and Sweden.

The survey, conducted on the Internet in November-December 2013, covered about 1,000 people aged 13-29 in each country.

Only 66.2 percent of Japanese respondents said they expect to feel happy when they are 40 years old, compared with 81.6 percent to 87.4 percent in the other countries.

The percentage of respondents who replied, "I am happy with myself" and "I have my good points" was the lowest in Japan as well, painting a picture of Japanese young people who are not confident in themselves and are pessimistic about the future.

The proportion of respondents who want to do something to help their own country was the highest in Japan at 54.5 percent. But the rate of Japanese who said their participation may have a positive impact on social change stood at 30.2 percent, the lowest among the seven.

---

> ### Report says young Japanese are not "satisfied" with themselves
>
> According to a recent report by the Japanese government, less than half of young people in Japan are satisfied with themselves. This is the lowest amount of youths surveyed in seven countries.
>
> The results of the survey are published in the annual white paper on the country's youth, released by the Cabinet Office on Tuesday. It contains the results of an online survey of people aged 13 to 29 in Japan, Britain, Germany, France, South Korea, Sweden and the United States. Responses were collected from some 7,400 youths in those countries.
>
> Although as many as 70 percent of young people in the other six countries said they were satisfied with themselves, that number was only 46 percent for youths in Japan. About 62 percent of Japanese youths reported having bright hopes for their future, in contrast to youths in the other six countries, where that number was over 80 percent.
>
> Even so, nearly 55 percent of the youths in Japan expressed a desire to do something to serve their country. This was the highest percentage of all the countries surveyed. The government report urged families, schools and community groups to create an encouraging and supportive environment that would enable children to develop positive feelings about themselves.

2. The articles report the results of the same survey but their focal points are somewhat different. Find similarities and differences between the two articles and write them in the table below. Compare your list with a partner.

| Similarities | Differences |
| --- | --- |
| | |

## 4 | Getting better at it — Language focus

### Reflection

What are some useful words or expressions in English that you used during this task?

What are some words or expressions in Japanese that you wanted to use, but you didn't know the English?

## 5 | Getting further — Extension

### Write a report to your boss

Integrate the information reported in the two articles and write a short summary that you will send to your boss.

## 6 | Getting it done — Wrap up

### Compare the surveys

Scan the QR code on the right side of the page and read the report of a similar survey on young people published in 2019. Some of the questions were identical to the ones in the articles you read in 3 **Getting into it**. Find similarities and differences between the two surveys and write them in the table below.

| Similarities | Differences |
|---|---|
|  |  |

## Unit 20 Deserted island

 **Goal** To decide what to bring to help you survive on a deserted island
無人島で生き残るために役立つものを決める

### 1 Getting warmed up

**Vocabulary building**

1. Write the word next to the description.

| | | | |
|---|---|---|---|
| slingshot | lighter | shovel | fishing rod |
| compass | hunting knife | saucepan | axe |

1. This is used for digging holes. _____

2. People use this for starting fires. _____

3. You can catch fish with this. _____

4. This can be used for cooking a meal. _____

5. This can be used to cut wood. _____

6. You can use this to shoot a stone at something. _____

7. This will help you to find your direction. _____

8. You can use this to kill an animal and get its skin. _____

2. Speak with your partner. Have you ever used any of these? If so, when?

### 2 Getting ready

**Creative thinking**

A necktie has many uses. For example:
- You can make a rope to walk your dog.
- You can use it as a bandage if you cut yourself.
- It can be used to tie the lid on a bento box.
- If you wrap your hands with it, you can pick up a hot pan from the oven.
- It can be a tail on a cat costume.

Work in a group. How many uses can you think of for a CD? Write as many as you can.

### 3 Getting into it

**Choose your survival items**

Imagine that your group is on a luxury cruise together. You are enjoying the trip, when suddenly, the ship hits a rock and starts to sink. You can see a small deserted island nearby, and you have a small boat to get there. The boat can hold your group and 15 kg of luggage.

What things will you take to the island? Firstly, make a list of the most important items. Secondly, speak together with your group and decide which things will be most useful for you. *Remember: the total weight must be less than 15 kg.*

| | | |
|---|---|---|
| 0.5kg | 3kg | 2kg |
| 1kg | 10kg | 3kg |
| 4kg | 0.5kg | 4kg |
| 0.5kg | 0.5kg | 0.5kg |
| 0.1kg | 8kg | 5kg |
| 2kg | 1kg | 2kg |
| 1kg | 2kg | |

Stage 1: My Top 5 Most Important Items

| Item | Reason why it is needed | |
|------|-------------------------|---|
| 1. | | |
| 2. | | |
| 3. | | |
| 4. | | |
| 5. | | |

Stage 2: Group discussion notes

_My group's final decision_

Items to take to the island:

Total weight:

## 4 | Getting better at it   〈 Language focus 〉

### Reflection

What are some words or expressions in English that were useful to complete this task?

What are some words or expressions in Japanese that you wanted to use, but couldn't?

Notes

## 5 Getting further  Extension

### Add your own ideas to the list

1. Think of three extra things you can take to the island that are not on your list. It can be anything you like. Think by yourself, and write some notes to help you explain to your group the reason why you want to take them.

Item 1: _____     Item 2: _____     Item 3: _____

Reason: _____     Reason: _____     Reason: _____

_____     _____     _____

_____     _____     _____

_____     _____     _____

2. Tell your group your ideas, and listen to everyone's suggestions. Then, choose together two extra items that your group will take to the island. Write them here:

Extra Item 1: _____     Extra Item 2: _____

## 6 Getting it done  Wrap up

### Write your survival story

Imagine that you and your group survived on the island for a month after the shipwreck. Write a short story for a magazine that explains how you survived, and *how you used some of the items you brought with you.*

_____

_____

_____

_____

_____

_____

_____

_____

_____

_____

_____

_____

_____

**Unit 21** **Amazing alumni**

**Goal** To evaluate candidates for an alumni award

「卒業生アワード」候補者を評価する

## 1 | Getting warmed up

### Vocabulary building

1. Draw a line to match a word with the description.

A person who...

| | |
|---|---|
| wealthy • | a. ...is very enthusiastic about something. |
| generous • | b. ...often breaks the rules. |
| rebellious • | c. ...is very interested in films, paintings, music and theater. |
| alcoholic • | d. ...has a lot of money. |
| passionate • | e. ...gives time and money to help people. |
| arty • | f. ...is addicted to wine and beer. |

2. Choose two words that are not on this list to describe your own personality. Tell your partner.

## 2 | Getting ready

### Talk about success

1. How important are these things for a happy and successful life? Circle your answer.

| | Not important | | | | Very important |
|---|---|---|---|---|---|
| a. having a lot of money | 1 | 2 | 3 | 4 | 5 |
| b. being married | 1 | 2 | 3 | 4 | 5 |
| c. having children | 1 | 2 | 3 | 4 | 5 |
| d. having lots of friends | 1 | 2 | 3 | 4 | 5 |
| e. being famous or well-known | 1 | 2 | 3 | 4 | 5 |
| f. doing volunteer work to help the community | 1 | 2 | 3 | 4 | 5 |

2. Compare your answers with a partner. What do you agree and disagree about?

 *The main task!*

## 3 | Getting into it

### Rank alumni award candidates

Your school will celebrate its 100th anniversary next year. As part of the celebrations, one past student will be chosen to receive a special award. This is a person who has contributed to raising the status and the reputation of your school. On the right page is a shortlist of candidates.

**Name:**
Tomoko Hara
Age: 63

### Achievements

Tomoko is a wealthy politician who has generously donated a lot of money to your school recently. Your school has a scholarship prize named after her. Tomoko enjoys much popularity and support from the community.

### Private life

Five years ago, the media discovered that she was having an affair, but she is still living with her husband now. Her son is working as an actor but is not very popular.

**Name:**
T.A.K.A.
Age: 35

### Achievements

T.A.K.A. is a hugely popular rap artist, with many teenage fans. He frequently collaborates with the world's top musicians. Many of his song lyrics express negative views about school and education.

### Private life

He is married to a famous movie actress. He has many tattoos on his arms.

**Name:**
Michiko Yamada
Age: 45

### Achievements

Michiko left her young son and husband in Japan and went to Africa to work as a medical doctor for 15 years. She helped to reduce poverty in Africa, adopting three young children and raising them herself. She has been praised by a number of international medical organisations.

### Private life

Michiko has almost no money in the bank and she doesn't have her own house or a car. She spent all her money to help poor people. She has a problem with alcohol.

**Name:**
Tetsuo Sato
Age: 53

### Achievements

Tetsuo played for many years as a professional soccer player, although he is now retired from sport and works as an instructor and commentator. He played in three Olympic games, as well as playing for one of the best soccer teams in Spain. He was known as a passionate and sometimes violent player.

### Private life

Although he was the captain of the school soccer team and performed very well, he hated studying and he was barely able to graduate.

**Name:**
Kantaro Murakami
Age: 75

### Achievements

Kantaro is a famous film director who has won national and international awards. He often gives lectures about films and he teaches an intensive film class at the National University of Art. He often appears on TV and in the media, giving insightful comments about social problems.

### Private life

He has a stubborn nature and a short temper, and so he is not liked by many actors. He is married to an actress who starred in his first film.

**Name:**
Melissa McGuire
Age: 68

### Achievements

Melissa was born in the UK and moved to Japan when she was five years old. She is a novelist who had a book on the New York Times Bestseller List. Her books have been very popular and have been translated into many different languages. She is well known all over the world.

### Private life

Melissa admitted that when she was a student, she hardly ever attended classes. She was more interested in working at her part-time job and hanging out in coffee shops. She has been divorced twice, and is now separated from her third husband.

1. Read through the descriptions of the candidates. Rank each person according to who should receive the award.

*My own opinion*

| Ranking | Name | Reason |
|---|---|---|
| 1 | | |
| 2 | | |
| 3 | | |
| 4 | | |
| 5 | | |
| 6 | | |

2. Work in a group. Share your rankings. Together, agree upon a ranking order.

Notes

_____

_____

_____

*My group's final decision*

| Ranking | Name | Reason |
|---|---|---|
| 1 | | |
| 2 | | |
| 3 | | |
| 4 | | |
| 5 | | |
| 6 | | |

## 4 | Getting better at it   ⌐ Language focus ⌐

### Reflection

What are some words or expressions in English that were useful to complete this task?

_____

_____

_____

_____

What are some words or expressions in Japanese that you wanted to use, but couldn't?

_____

_____

_____

_____

## 5 Getting further  ⟨ Extension ⟩

### Decide the prize

The top candidate will receive a special award, but the second- and third-placed candidates will also be given a prize in recognition of their achievements.

1. Think of three prizes that are suitable for each of the Top 3 candidates. The prize can be anything, for example: money, a trip overseas, their name on a school building, a trophy, or your own original idea. Write your opinion here:

*My own opinion*

| Ranking | Name | Prize | Reason |
|---------|------|-------|--------|
| 1 | | | |
| 2 | | | |
| 3 | | | |

2. Work in a group. Share your ideas. Together, decide upon a prize for each candidate.

*My group's decision*

| Ranking | Name | Prize | Reason |
|---------|------|-------|--------|
| 1 | | | |
| 2 | | | |
| 3 | | | |

## 6 Getting it done  ⟨ Wrap up ⟩

### Write a recommendation

On a separate piece of paper, write a recommendation to the school board for the alumni awards. In your letter:

1. Tell the board your group's Top 3 candidates for the award.
2. Explain the reason why your group chose those three people.
3. Suggest a prize for each of those three candidates.

## 22 | Group trip

**Goal** To decide the best place to stay for a group holiday
グループ旅行に最適な宿泊場所を決める

### 1 | Getting warmed up

**Reflect on your priorities**

1. When planning a vacation, what are the most important points to consider in choosing a place to stay? Rank the following points in order of importance.

- Price
- Amenities (fridge, dryer, Wi-Fi, etc.)
- Cleanliness
- Staff/host
- Location/access

Ranking
1. [                          ] — Most important
2. [                          ]
3. [                          ]
4. [                          ]
5. [                          ] — Least important

2. Work in a pair or a group. Explain your ranking and give reasons for your decision. Do you agree or disagree with your partner's opinions?

### 2 | Getting ready

**Evaluate the options for accommodation**

Get a worksheet from your teacher. Imagine that you are going to Hawaii for one week for a group holiday. You are planning to rent an apartment there.

**PART A**

1. Work individually and evaluate the three accommodations on the worksheet. Check the appropriate box (✔) in the following categories: poor (×), average (△), and excellent (○).

| | Apartment in Kona | | | Apartment in Honolulu | | | Treehouse at Kilauea Volcano | | |
|---|---|---|---|---|---|---|---|---|---|
| | × | △ | ○ | × | △ | ○ | × | △ | ○ |
| Price | | | | | | | | | |
| Amenities | | | | | | | | | |
| Cleanliness | | | | | | | | | |
| Staff/host | | | | | | | | | |
| Location/access | | | | | | | | | |
| Comments (if any) | | | | | | | | | |

2. Make a personal choice from among the three accommodations as to where you would prefer to stay.

**Your choice:** _____

PART B

Search on the Internet for more information about Hawaii that would be useful to decide the best place to stay (e.g. locations of cities and islands, flight routes from Japan, sightseeing spots). After searching, you can change the accommodation you selected in Part A, if necessary.

*The main task!*

## 3 Getting into it

### Discuss the best place to stay

Work in a group. Which accommodation is the best option for a group holiday? Evaluate all the options together first, discussing the pros and cons of each place, and then decide. Write at least three reasons for your group's choice.

**The group's choice:** _____

Reasons:

- _____
- _____
- _____

## 4 Getting better at it  *Language focus*

### Reflection

What are some words or expressions in English that were useful to complete this task?

_____

_____

_____

What are some words or expressions in Japanese that you wanted to use, but couldn't?

_____

_____

_____

Attach your sheet here.

Notes

## 5 Getting further  — Extension

### Task repetition

1. Work in a group. You are planning to go abroad for a week for a group holiday. Where would you like to go? Decide one place.
2. Search on the Internet by yourself and prepare an option (options) for accommodation.
3. Share your choice with other members of your group and decide the best place to stay.

## 6 Getting it done  — Wrap up

### Write a report

Summarize what you discussed in 5 **Getting further**. Write about your travel destination and the place where you decided to stay. Explain the reasons why your group chose that place.

Travel destination: _____   Place to stay: _____

Reasons:

- _____
- _____
- _____

*memo*

## Unit 23 | Top timetable

**Goal** To create the perfect timetable
理想の時間割を作る

### 1 Getting warmed up

音声ページ

**Listen and complete the timetable**

Listen to audio of a teacher explaining the timetable below. There are five differences between the explanation and the timetable. Listen carefully and identify the differences.

| | Time | Monday | Tuesday | Wednesday | Thursday | Friday |
|---|---|---|---|---|---|---|
| | 8:20 ~ 8:40 | SHR | | | | |
| 1 | 8:50 ~ 9:40 | Japanese History A | English Expression I | Basic Biology | Classics | Contemporary Japanese Language |
| 2 | 9:50 ~ 10:40 | Math A | PE | World History A | Math A | Math I |
| 3 | 10:50 ~ 11:40 | Japanese History A | Contemporary Japanese Language | English Expression I | Basic Biology | World History A |
| 4 | 11:50 ~ 12:40 | Classics | Basic Biology | Information Study I | Health | Information Study I |
| | 12:40 ~ 13:30 | Lunchtime | | | | |
| 5 | 13:30 ~ 14:20 | Contemporary Japanese Language | Math I | PE | English Expression I | Health |
| 6 | 14:30 ~ 15:20 | English Communication I | Classics | Inquiry-Based Cross-Disciplinary Study | Japanese History A | English Communication I |
| | 15:25 ~ 15:35 | Meditation | | | | |
| 7 | 15:40 ~ 16:30 | LHR | | | | |

*Notes.* SHR = Short homeroom, LHR = Long homeroom, PE = Physical education.

## 2 | Getting ready

### Reflect on your values

1. The sample timetable on the left page was created for first-year students at high school. What do you think are the good and bad points of the schedule?

| Good points | Bad points |
| --- | --- |
| | |

2. Work in a group. Share your list with other members. Do you agree or disagree with their opinions?

3. Work in a group. What do you think is essential for the perfect timetable? (e.g. Students need enough time to do exercise.)

- 
- 
- 
- 
- 
- 
- 
- 
- 

## 3 | Getting into it

### Create the perfect timetable

Work in a group. Create the perfect timetable for first-year students at high school.

(Continued on the next page.)

*(Use this table for your personal notes.)*

| | Time | Monday | Tuesday | Wednesday | Thursday | Friday | |
|---|---|---|---|---|---|---|---|
| | | | | | | | |
| | | | | | | | |
| | | | | | | | |
| | | | | | | | |
| | | | | | | | |
| | | | | | | | |
| | | | | | | | |
| | | | | | | | |
| | | | | | | | |
| | | | | | | | |

Notes

## 4 | Getting better at it — *Language focus*

### Reflection

What are some words or expressions in English that were useful to complete this task?

What are some words or expressions in Japanese that you wanted to use, but couldn't?

Notes

**5** **Getting further** $\langle$ Extension $\rangle$

### Create a new subject

1. Work individually. Considering the knowledge and skills that people need to be successful in life, what new subject could you create to be taught in high school? Name the subject, describe the goals and content of the subject, and explain the reason(s) why it is necessary.

Subject name : _____

Goals and content

Reason(s) why it is necessary

2. Share your ideas in a group and choose one of the best ideas. Then, replace one of the class periods in your group's timetable with the new subject.

**6** **Getting it done** $\langle$ Wrap up $\rangle$

### Evaluate timetables

Look at the timetables created by other groups. Take notes of the other groups' ideas in the table below. Make some comments about the good ideas, the surprising ideas, and anything else that you think is important or noteworthy.

| Ideas | Comments |
|---|---|
|  |  |

## Unit 24 | Agony Aunt

Goal **To give advice for some problems**
悩み相談に対して解決策を提示する

### 1 | Getting warmed up

**Consider some advice**

An Agony Aunt is a person who writes a column in a magazine, giving advice to readers who have written in with their personal problems.

Work in a pair. Read the column below. Do you think the Agony Aunt gave good advice? Why or why not? Share your ideas with the class.

---

Dear Agony Aunt,

My best friend and I have known each other since we were eight years old. I enjoy her company, but she is not good at keeping secrets. She often tells people my embarrassing stories from childhood. I have told her many times not to tell my secrets to other people, but she can't stop doing it. What should I do? Should we stop being friends?

Polly Private

---

Dear Polly,

I am sorry to hear that your best friend cannot keep your secrets. My advice is to tell her how you feel when she shares your secrets with others. If she still doesn't stop, then you should stop being friends. If she doesn't respect your privacy and continues to hurt you, she is not a true friend.

Agony Aunt

---

## 2 | Getting ready

### Give some advice

Work in a pair. Imagine that you are an Agony Aunt. Read the question from Troubled Teenager, and discuss what advice you could give. Think of as many ideas as you can. Then, share your ideas with the class.

Dear Agony Aunt,

There is a girl in my chemistry class that I really like. She is very pretty and always looks cheerful when she is talking with her friends. I have never talked to her, and sadly, she doesn't seem to know I exist. I want to get to know her, but I am too shy and do not know how to talk to girls. What should I do?

Troubled Teenager

*The main task!*

## 3 | Getting into it

### Write an advice column

1. Work in a pair. Your teacher will give you a sheet with four questions that magazine readers wrote to Agony Aunt. Imagine that you are Agony Aunt. Read the questions, and think of some good advice for the problems.

2. Write a reply to give advice to each problem.

(1)

(2)

Attach your sheet here.

(3)

_____

_____

_____

_____

(4)

_____

_____

_____

_____

3. Share your advice with the class. Choose the best advice for each problem.

## 4 | Getting better at it  ⟨ Language focus ⟩

### Reflection

What are some words or expressions in English that were useful to complete this task?

What are some words or expressions in Japanese that you wanted to use, but couldn't?

Notes

**5** **Getting further** ⟨*Extension*⟩

**Ask for advice**

1. Think of a problem that you or someone you know has. Write a letter to Agony Aunt asking for advice.

_____

_____

_____

_____

_____

_____

_____

2. Make a pair. Listen to your partner read his/her letter. Then, give your partner some advice. After that, swap roles and do it again.

**6** **Getting it done** ⟨*Wrap up*⟩

**Write a reply**

Write a reply giving advice for your partner's problem in **5** **Getting further**.

Summary of your partner's problem:

_____

_____

_____

Your reply:

_____

_____

_____

_____

_____

_____

_____

_____

# Appendix

# Self-assessment rubrics

# Useful words and expressions

# Self-assessment rubrics

## Unit 1. Fantastic flags

| | | | |
|---|---|---|---|
| **2 Getting ready** How many national flags did you and your partner identify? | No. _____ | | |
| **3 Getting into it** and **5 Getting further** When you were a director, could you say more than 3 things to describe the flag? | × | △ | ○ |
| Did you use English all the time when required? | × | △ | ○ |
| How satisfied are you with your performance on the task? | × | △ | ○ |

Compared to other members in your group, what were your strong (weak) points?

## Unit 2. Picture this scene

| | | | |
|---|---|---|---|
| Did you successfully describe your picture to your partner? | × | △ | ○ |
| Did you successfully draw the items in your partner's picture? | × | △ | ○ |
| Did you use English all the time when required? | × | △ | ○ |
| Did you learn some new phrases or vocabulary during this lesson? | × | △ | ○ |

When you compare the picture you received from the teacher with the picture that your partner actually drew, how could you describe it differently to make the drawing better?

## Unit 3. Putting things in place

| | | |
|---|---|---|
| **3** **Getting into it** How many items <u>were you</u> / <u>was your partner</u> able to add to the picture? | | /23 |
| **5** **Getting further** How many items <u>were you</u> / <u>was your partner</u> able to describe from the picture? | | /23 |
| Did you use English all the time when required? | | × △ ○ |
| Did you use phrases and sentences, not just single words? | | × △ ○ |

How can you improve your performance next time?

## Unit 4. Spot the difference

| | | |
|---|---|---|
| **3** **Getting into it** How many differences did you find? | | /10 |
| Did you successfully describe your picture to your partner? | | × △ ○ |
| Did you use English all the time when required? | | × △ ○ |
| Did you use phrases and sentences, not just single words? | | × △ ○ |

What strategies helped you to successfully find the differences?

## Unit 5. Put a name to the desk

| | |
|---|---|
| **3 Getting into it** How many of the desks did you successfully identify? | /8 |

| | | | |
|---|---|---|---|
| **5 Getting further** How satisfied are you with your performance on the task? | ✕ | △ | ○ |
| Did you use phrases and sentences, and not just single words? | ✕ | △ | ○ |
| Did you learn some new phrases or vocabulary during this lesson? | ✕ | △ | ○ |

How will you do this task differently next time?

## Unit 6. Get your story straight

| | |
|---|---|
| **3 Getting into it** How many differences did you find? | No._____ |

| | | | |
|---|---|---|---|
| **5 Getting further** Were you able to tell an interesting story? | ✕ | △ | ○ |
| Did you use phrases and sentences, not just single words? | ✕ | △ | ○ |
| Were you able to explain the reasons for your opinions? | ✕ | △ | ○ |

The next time you tell a story, how can you improve your performance?

## Unit 7. Lie through your teeth

| | | | |
|---|---|---|---|
| **3 Getting into it** and **5 Getting further** How many lies did you correctly guess? | | | |
| **3 Getting into it** and **5 Getting further** How many people did you successfully deceive? | | | |
| Did you use phrases and sentences, not just single words? | × | △ | ○ |
| How satisfied are you with your performance on the task? | × | △ | ○ |

Compared to other members in your group, what were your strong/weak points?

## Unit 8. After the quake

| | | | |
|---|---|---|---|
| When you explained the condition of the room, were you able to give specific (detailed) descriptions? | × | △ | ○ |
| Generally, were your guesses correct? | × | △ | ○ |
| Did you use phrases and sentences, not just single words in your descriptions? | × | △ | ○ |
| Did you express your ideas clearly? | × | △ | ○ |

Based on your performance, what were your strong and weak points when communicating in English?

## Unit 9. Search for something in common

| | | | |
|---|---|---|---|
| Did you find out interesting things about your classmates? | × | △ | ○ |
| When you wanted to know more information about your classmates, did you ask extra questions? | × | △ | ○ |
| Did you use natural expressions to complete the task? | × | △ | ○ |
| Did you learn some new phrases or vocabulary during this lesson? | × | △ | ○ |

How would you do this task differently next time?

## Unit 10. Chicken pot pie

| | | | |
|---|---|---|---|
| 2 **Getting ready** How many pictures did you get in the correct order? | | /6 | |
| 3 **Getting into it** How many pictures did you get in the correct order? | | /10 | |
| Did you use phrases and sentences, and not just single words? | × | △ | ○ |
| Did you respond appropriately to other people's ideas? | × | △ | ○ |

Based on your performance, what were your weak points when communicating in English?

## Unit 11. Life in a train carriage

| | | | |
|---|---|---|---|
| **3** **Getting into it** Did your pair successfully put the pictures in order? | × | △ | ○ |
| Did you successfully describe your pictures to your partner? | × | △ | ○ |
| Did you use English all the time when required? | × | △ | ○ |
| Did you learn some new phrases or vocabulary during this lesson? | × | △ | ○ |

What did you find most difficult about this lesson?

## Unit 12. The suspicious mother

| | | | |
|---|---|---|---|
| Did you put the lines in the correct order? | × | △ | ○ |
| Were you able to understand the completed story? | × | △ | ○ |
| Did you use English all the time when required? | × | △ | ○ |
| Did you express your ideas clearly? | × | △ | ○ |

What did you find most difficult about this lesson?

## Unit 13. Catch the criminal

| | Yes/No | | |
|---|---|---|---|
| Did you guess the criminal correctly? | Yes/No | | |
| Were you able to understand the story? | × | △ | ○ |
| Did you use English all the time when required? | × | △ | ○ |
| Did you express your ideas clearly? | × | △ | ○ |

Compared to other members in your group, what were your strong (weak) points?

## Unit 14. Storytelling with cartoons

| | | | |
|---|---|---|---|
| **1** **Getting warmed up** Were you able to correctly guess your partner's boxes? | × | △ | ○ |
| **3** **Getting into it** How many parts of the story did you (or your partner) repeat correctly? | /10 | | |
| Did you use phrases and sentences, not just single words? | × | △ | ○ |
| Did you use natural expressions to complete the task? | × | △ | ○ |

Compared to your partner, what were your strong (weak) points?

## Unit 15. Storytelling with videos

| | | | |
|---|---|---|---|
| Could you explain what was happening without long pauses or silences, keeping in time with the pace of the story? | × | △ | ○ |
| Apart from the characters' actions, were you also able to describe their feelings and the setting of the story? | × | △ | ○ |
| Did you use phrases and sentences, not just single words? | × | △ | ○ |
| How satisfied are you with your performance on the task? | × | △ | ○ |

How could you improve your performance next time?

## Unit 16. Figure out the puzzle

| | | | |
|---|---|---|---|
| Even if you didn't know the solution to a puzzle, were you able to express some ideas and contribute to the discussion? | × | △ | ○ |
| When explaining a possible solution, were you able to clearly express your thinking and explain the reasons? | × | △ | ○ |
| Did you use phrases and sentences, not just single words? | × | △ | ○ |
| Did you use English all the time when required? | × | △ | ○ |

What did you find most difficult about this lesson?

## Unit 17. Figure out the relationships

| | |
|---|---|
| **1 Getting warmed up** How many names did you get correct? | /13 |

| | | | |
|---|---|---|---|
| **3 Getting into it** Did you correctly figure out the character relationships? | × | △ | ○ |
| Did you contribute useful ideas to the discussion? | × | △ | ○ |
| Did you respond appropriately to other people's ideas? | × | △ | ○ |

Compared to other members in your group, what were your strong (weak) points?

## Unit 18. Origami challenge

| | | | |
|---|---|---|---|
| Did you successfully make the origami? | × | △ | ○ |
| Did you learn some new phrases or vocabulary during this lesson? | × | △ | ○ |
| Did you use English all the time when required? | × | △ | ○ |
| How satisfied are you with your performance on the task? | × | △ | ○ |

How will you do this task differently next time?

## Unit 19. Japanese life satisfaction

| | |
|---|---|
| **3** **Getting into it** How many *differences* did you find? | No._____ |
| **3** **Getting into it** How many *similarities* did you find? | No._____ |

| | | | |
|---|---|---|---|
| Did you learn some new phrases or vocabulary during this lesson? | × | △ | ○ |
| Did you express your ideas clearly? | × | △ | ○ |

What did you learn from this lesson?

## Unit 20. Deserted island

| | |
|---|---|
| **2** **Getting ready** How many uses did you think of for a CD? | No._____ |

| | | | |
|---|---|---|---|
| **3** **Getting into it** Did you agree or disagree with other people's opinions? | × | △ | ○ |
| Were you able to explain the reasons for your opinions? | × | △ | ○ |
| Did you learn some new phrases or vocabulary during this lesson? | × | △ | ○ |

Are you satisfied with the items your group chose to take to the island? Why or why not?

## Unit 21. Amazing alumni

| | × | △ | ○ |
|---|---|---|---|
| Were you able to argue the reasons for your ranking decision? | × | △ | ○ |
| Were you able to agree and disagree with other peoples' opinions? | × | △ | ○ |
| Did you learn some new phrases or vocabulary during this lesson? | × | △ | ○ |
| How satisfied are you with your performance on the task? | × | △ | ○ |

What advice would you give someone who is doing a discussion task like this one?

## Unit 22. Group trip

| | × | △ | ○ |
|---|---|---|---|
| **3** **Getting into it** Were you able to decide a place to stay that satisfied everyone? | × | △ | ○ |
| **5** **Getting further** Were you able to decide a place to stay that satisfied everyone? | × | △ | ○ |
| Were you able to explain the reasons for your opinions? | × | △ | ○ |
| Did you use English all the time when required? | × | △ | ○ |

What did you learn from this lesson?

## Unit 23. Top timetable

| | /5 | | |
|---|---|---|---|
| **1 Getting warmed up** How many differences did you find? | | | |
| Did your group successfully create an ideal timetable? | × | △ | ○ |
| How satisfied are you with your performance on the task? | × | △ | ○ |
| Were you able to explain the reasons for your opinions? | × | △ | ○ |

Based on your performance, what were your strong and weak points when communicating in English?

## Unit 24. Agony Aunt

| | | | |
|---|---|---|---|
| Did you come up with a lot of advice for each problem? | × | △ | ○ |
| Were you able to give helpful advice? | × | △ | ○ |
| Did you express your ideas clearly? | × | △ | ○ |
| Were you able to explain the reasons for your opinions? | × | △ | ○ |

How can you improve your performance next time?

# Useful words and expressions

## Unit 1 Fantastic flags

stripe

thick/thin line

sun

crescent moon

star

cross

'X' shape

rectangle

square

circle

triangle

point

Union Jack

image

picture

background

a half/third

horizontal/vertical

diagonal

top/middle/bottom

left/center/right

touch the edge

divide in half

divide into thirds

top left corner

bottom right corner

a line at 45 (90) degrees

## Unit 2 Picture this scene

He/She is wearing ...

He/She is in ... (e.g. a dress)

He/She is talking with ...

He/She is holding ...

the woman with ...

the man/woman who ...

He/She is standing next to/by/in front of/behind ...

There is/are ...

## Unit 3 Putting things in place

cutting board

jug

cupboard

sink

chandelier lights

food mixer

spatula

soup ladle

paper towel roll

cactus

a loaf of bread

a pile of plates

a basket of fruit

a carton of milk

hanging on the left/middle/right hook

on the left/right of ...

... to the left/right of ...

on the top/bottom shelf of ...

in the corner

above/below ...

between ... and ...

in the middle of ...

## Unit 4 Spot the difference

*Grocery store*

shelf

clerk

apron

purse

carpet

meat counter

stool

have fallen out of the box

mops

brooms

**Family dinner**
fork
spoon
wearing a tie
on the right/left
next to ...
in front of ...
playing with his phone

**Spanish fiesta**
doorknob
bald
long sleeves
beard
on the near/far balcony
in the bottom right/left corner
on the far wall
There is/are ...

## Unit 5   Put a name to the desk

on/under the desk
on the left/right of the desk
in the middle of the desk
hanging on the chair

a lot of stuff / heaps of stuff
a mess (messy)
tidy
organized

## Unit 6   Get your story straight

**Comparing stories**
This one has simpler language.
That one is aimed at a more mature
   audience.
Your story sounds more suspenseful/
   humorous/complex.
This story has a lot of dialogue.
That is more descriptive.

My story focuses on character.

**Telling stories**
Once upon a time ...
A long time ago ...
There was a man/woman who ...
One day, ...
... and they all lived happily ever after.

## Unit 7   Lie through your teeth

**When telling a story**
You're not going to believe this, but ...
I swear it's the truth.
I'm not kidding.
It really happened.

**When spotting a lie**
You're kidding.
No way!
That sounds a bit fishy to me.

## Unit 8   After the quake

**Picture 2: After a level 5 earthquake**
dog wakes up
some books fall off the shelves
a book hits the father on the head
some bottles fall off the shelf
TV turns off
little boy stops laughing
drinks on the table tip over
plates are broken
glasses in the cabinet fall over
some plates break
grandmother is shocked

**Picture 3: After a level 6 earthquake**
bookshelf falls over
walls are cracked
toy falls off the top of the bookshelf
some lights are cracked (or smashed)
more books fall off the bookshelf
children hide under the table
grandmother puts her hands over her
   eyes
chairs fall over
knife falls near mother's feet
pot falls off the stove

tomato falls onto the floor

top cupboard door opens

all the glasses in the cabinet are smashed

*Picture 4: After a level 7 earthquake*

dog escapes

house collapses

electricity pole falls over

windows are broken (smashed)

roof tiles are broken

walls are cracked

house sinks into the ground

house becomes a pile of rubble

## Unit 9   Search for something in common

I did too!

Me too.

The same for me.

Is it the same for you, too?

No, not me.

We all used to ... when we were in high
   school.

All of us enjoy ...

Three of us are ...

Two of us often ...

## Unit 10   Chicken pot pie

The first (second/third) picture

pour

cover

until it becomes soft

slowly add

take it off the heat

put aside

boil

## Unit 11   Life in a train carriage

I guess ... comes first.

This order could be wrong.

Why don't we check our answers?

I can see ...

have an argument

passenger

hold on to the rail

hold on to the strap

It started raining outside.

give up one's seat for ...

get off the train

hang one's umbrella on the rail

drop ... on ...

train conductor

pick up

after a while

## Unit 12   The suspicious mother

Where does this line belong?

The last word of this line is ... (e.g. "the"),
   so the first word of the next line must
   be ... (e.g. a noun)

This must follow ...

Could you read that again?

What do you think comes next?

What does this word mean?

That doesn't make sense.

## Unit 13   Catch the criminal

... must have been angry with ... because ...

... may/must have killed the victim.

That makes sense.

That would make sense if ...

If that's true, then ...

That's the reason why ...

I don't understand why he ...

Tell me again about your suspect.

Who do you think the murderer is?

You may be right about that, but ...

I guess you could be right.

## Unit 14  Storytelling with cartoons

*Wet paint*

old door

poor condition

paint

children

playing

dog

wanted to go inside

scratched

shocked

ball

hit

ran into the door

made dirty marks

upset

*Ants*

ant

gathering food

ants' nest

a line

was squashed/crushed

dirt

dead bodies

washed away

cookie

a piece

a flood

## Unit 15  Storytelling with videos

*English for Beginners*

elderly man

online shopping

delivery truck

a kettle boils

put sticky notes

wear headphones

repeat the words

snore

hug

granddaughter

*Shaun the Fugitive*

farm house

smash cakes

peek through a window

slip and fall down

tractor

pink icing

run away

footprints

give instructions

strangle

step back

hide

scarecrow

rubber gloves

surrounded

fix

replace a pipe

tighten a bolt

start the engine

pat ... on the head

## Unit 16  Figure out the puzzle

*Presenting an answer*

Well, firstly ...

To begin with, ...

I'd start by ...

For a start, ...

There're two points here. Firstly, ...
   Secondly, ...

There are two problems here ...
   Moreover ...

You also have to consider ...

*Expressing an opinion*

In my opinion, ...

In my view, ...

I reckon ...

I definitely think that ...

*Agreeing in part*

Yes, perhaps, however ...

Well, yes, but ...
Hmm, possibly, but ...
Yes, I agree up to a point, however ...
Well, you have a point there, but ...
There's something there, I suppose,
    however ...

*Asking for clarification*
You lost me there.
I'm lost.
I'm not following.
I didn't get that.
What do you mean?

What do you mean by ...?
What are you trying to say?
In what way?
How do you mean?

*Explaining*
What I mean is ...
What I'm saying is ...
What I'm trying to say is ...
Don't get me wrong ...
Don't misunderstand me ...
Let me put it another way, ...

## Unit 17   Figure out the relationships

perhaps
probably
I think that / It seems to me that
That would be interesting.

Because ... I suppose that ...
As ... happened in the past, it caused ...
That's an interesting idea!
Let's use that idea.

## Unit 18   Origami challenge

color side
edge
diamond
corner
pentagon
top/bottom half
octagon
squash fold
tip

fold
unfold
crease
turn over
put on
in half
flap
press flat
meet in the center

## Unit 19   Japanese life satisfaction

A is different from B
A is similar to B
In contrast to A, B is ...
Compared with A, ...
Similarly, ...

Likewise, ...
In the same way ...,
... while ...
... whereas ...

## Unit 20   Deserted island

It can be used for ...ing
We can use it to ...
I think it will come in handy.
That's a good idea.

I'm not sure about that.
That's pretty useless.
I think this is a waste of space.

## Unit 21   Amazing alumni

*Giving your opinion*
It seems to me that ...
In my view, ...
I definitely think that ...
Well, if you ask me, ...

*Agreeing*
That's so true!

I couldn't agree with you more.
That's exactly what I think.

*Disagreeing*
I'm afraid I can't agree.
I'm not sure about that.
I see what you mean, but ...

## Unit 22   Group trip

(un)comfortable
(in)convenient
pricey
... is highly recommended for this price.
How about the location?
... is centrally located.

... is close to ...
... is far from ...
I need a hair dryer.
... should be better.
safe/dangerous
... has a good reputation.

## Unit 23   Top timetable

... will be necessary in the future.
... is unnecessary.
It would be interesting if ...
... should be useful if ...
I should have studied ...
Students may want to ...

start later
end earlier
... is short/long.
How about ...
change the order of ...
... is a great idea.

## Unit 24   Agony Aunt

*Asking for advice*
What should I do (about ...)?
What do you think I should do (about ...)?
What do you suggest I do (about ...)?
Could you recommend ...?

*Giving advice*
If I were you, I would ...
I think you should ...
Why don't you ...?
I would advise you to ...
You might try ...
Focus on what is important.
Tell him how you feel.

Get your priorities in order.
Honesty is the best policy.

*Common sayings for advice (aphorisms)*
Don't judge a book by its cover.
Every cloud has a silver lining.
Practice what you preach.
Honesty is the best policy.
There is a light at the end of the tunnel.
Actions speak louder than words.
If it isn't broken, don't fix it.
The squeaky wheel gets the grease.
When in Rome, do as the Romans do.

編著者

田村　祐（たむら　ゆう）関西大学外国語学部

Paul Wicking（ポール・ウィキン）名城大学外国語学部

著者

横山友里（よこやま　ゆり）中京大学グローバル教育センター

松村昌紀（まつむら　まさのり）名城大学理工学部

小林真実（こばやし　まなみ）中京大学グローバル教育センター

加藤由崇（かとう　よしたか）中部大学人間力創成教育院

## タスクで教室から世界へ ［ブック2］

2023 年 2 月 20 日　第 1 版発行
2024 年 3 月 20 日　第 2 版発行

| | |
|---|---|
| 編 著 者 | 田村　祐・Paul Wicking |
| 著　　者 | 横山友里・松村昌紀・小林真実・加藤由崇 |
| 発 行 者 | 前田俊秀 |
| 発 行 所 | 株式会社 三修社 |
| | 〒 150-0001 東京都渋谷区神宮前 2-2-22 |
| | TEL03-3405-4511 |
| | FAX03-3405-4522 |
| | 振替 00190-9-72758 |
| | https://www.sanshusha.co.jp |
| | 編集担当　三井るり子 |
| 印 刷 所 | 広研印刷株式会社 |

©2023 Printed in Japan ISBN978-4-384-33518-7 C1082

表紙・本文デザイン＆DTP
　　　　　　　　　川原田良一（ロビンソン・ファクトリー）
本文イラスト　　初村フェルナンド
音声製作　　　　高速録音株式会社（録音 ELEC）